fluttertongue 4

adagio for the pressured surround

*for Bert,
in honour of our passing
habitations - Toronto, Lethbridge*

STEVEN ROSS SMITH

Steven.

March. 2017.

Library and Archives Canada Cataloguing in Publication
Smith, Steven, 1945-
Fluttertongue 4 : adagio for the pressured surround / Steven Ross Smith.

A poem.
ISBN 978-1-897126-12-7

I. Title. II. Title: Fluttertongue four.

PS8587.M59F584 2007   C811'.54   C2007-900199-8

Editor for the press: Douglas Barbour
Cover and interior design: Katherine Melnyk
Cover image: "Making a Connection," mixed mediums, by Jane Murray
Author Photo: Tammy Boehmer

NeWest Press acknowledges the support of the Canada Council for the Arts and the Alberta Foundation for the Arts, and the Edmonton Arts Council for our publishing program. We also acknowledge the financial support of the Government of Canada through the Book Publishing Industry Development Program (BPIDP) for our publishing activities.

NeWest Press
201–8540–109 Street
Edmonton, Alberta T6G 1E6
(780) 432-9427
www.newestpress.com

1 2 3 4 5 10 09 08 07

PRINTED AND BOUND IN CANADA

We are living particles, fireflies in the world, and around us resounds an enormous concert of noise-and-rumor-producing machines, creating a din and rumors destined to ensure we don't hear the voice of truth. But the interior enemies are just as numerous. It concerns our fear: this is what we are made of: our weakness.

Hélène Cixous

My father's wings, and his before him
vast inner
fluttering

Colin Browne

A mossfringed grove. above, an eagle circles. stretches a talon to scratch her underwing, plucks, from her body, setting adrift, a single white feather.

feather floats, as she thermals up. away.

feather, current-borne, hollow-shafted — cleft, wordless.

utterance is loss.

(my) Father, a roil of words.

loss unutterable.

a crumbling shore. breaking sky.

forage for words. store them in cloth pockets, in satchels, in every room of my house. they fall away. from every stitch and seam. from every clasp.

9. on the verge of
a phrasing of birds awing in the grove. wrentit chatter-rattles. chickadee, warbler, towhee. scuffle and trill.

ears atingle with chitter and chat. i sit still.

eagle-shadow whispers in moss and fern.

eagle-thought.

try to imagine.

i know (my) Father well, but He is a mystery. so too the
white-headed minds of baldies skirting islands and coast-lines.

lines, coastal, edging toward. hunger draws.

17.   *I figure if you start at "A" you can't go wrong.*
       love bp. Supper March 9th '87

wave-worn rock, the pressured surround.

strand/ed choice. islanded. skittery. at sea, pretending calm.

sea, steely blue almost white   at high tide   licking rocky outcrops.
land-limbs.

arm jars a cup.

spillage.

the poem splashing over the rim of definition.

miles away in a hard glinty room Evelyn is hardly eating. or
speaking. her (voice) chemo'd, empty.

such staining, and words.

i am a beggar, circling a lack.

trawling for diction, syntax. coarse or airy wordpour. currentflow.
lines to coast on.

featherdrift. white-crowned sparrow   high in spruce   above the
chain saw's biting descant   trills.

ferry queen hovers and spills travellers.

motorrumble throbs from the hull up through rock hollows and
breaks in the trees, into the island full of dream-balm mulled from
twenty-six herbs and stones.

pulsing in my ribcage i am spun, dizzied by water's surround.

the practice of torture twisting through centuries.

33.   her (voice) a bare whisper her husband, (my) Father, cannot hear.
       loss-fringed. lapping deficit. He strains after syllables that vanish
       into the dark unheard.

whispering *drink me* words evaporate.

i am His blood but not His cochlea.

salt grits in furrows of my forehead, creases of neck.

parched   mouth.

the wound makes itself known.

not reading, lips or symbols. stranded.

scavenging an inkdrop, squeezing featherdry alphabet for juice.

can't hear for Him.

42.   chainsaw gnaws. whiny raga in cellulose.

from the path, between arbutus and oak, a spilling of dogs and
strangers with accents. and questions.

discreet. hand covering my name.

nice day. restrained.

decipher, hedge.

under tongue-cover (we) invent identities.

are characters we read. stories of gamblers, of penchants for confession, asphyxia.

what can *i* assume of *we*?

enter to win.

rooms, raffles. the day.

the contest poem is an underfed dog.

i'd be reading right now but for this — (you, now reading) — but for strangers.

the lure of letters dangled, floating.

serif-hook. dog-slouch.

i'm Gullivered by stakes and loops. loss-adorned.

pressured. a membranous sac.

the pronoun is who?

squirm, beg mercy. search and search for self in mystery that pattern might reveal. confess to anything.

blind turning. hand slackens. the game stacks.

because of Emmett's skin, because his skin's vulnerability is terrifying.

recombinant DNAlphabet derives me. drives. desires. ravished by erased codes. cast neither this nor that way, by my own encryption.

63.   maze. a white-tipped sea. dog-tail wagging a lazy farewell through the gate.

marker day. transition. trace. five and a half decades falling away. enumeration. annum versary. this scribble. talon-scratch. poke of dark symbols across the island i am.

surrounded by years, self-looped in trees. bush and moss cushion shores. and here, a stump, a rock. a grazed shin. a breath in the philosopher's grove.

words should come to ease, shaped as great thoughts.

islanded among salal and cedar. near foxglove, yellow warbler, i'm a-buzz.

exhaled thought-pulse, sputtering from a small space. surrounded by sea and land. and flesh that falls away.

that fallen tree is an archway. a lover's arching back, a vowel.

tongued exchange slips through in memory. and time. through and up. slope-climber.

in peaking. a cry. ecstatic life-vowel.

oh. h-h-h-h-h. breathe into the rock.

i land. circling. can't remember a quarter century. can circle the day. on a grid. in mind.

74. or back in time see (my) son born and self-in-him borne from his straining miraculous mother into this world and see the island forming from the sea and see his self becoming and forget all loss.

buoyed and wordless. boyed.

above, a circling of eagles.

the buzzing itself is not annoying. i wake up about now anyway. to lumps and blockages.

sun a low blaze, molten through trees.

i have read a few thousand words since rising, to free them.

was it wind calling? tires on gravelled road? the pressure?

81.   between two mountains, here on the slope of one, looking up at the cedar with a forking trunk, the wound is a small ache below the branching.

syntax adapts. forks the poem.

avoiding the prescribed, you can forget sex. almost.

concentration. avoidance, or avowal? sea lions snort and belly up onto the rocks. point of view. rubber torpedoes.

Evelyn surrounded by machines.

anchor-weight, down-draft. a small *h*.

she's eating little.

a friend of mine doesn't eat, but she is young and her body keeps going.

self torturing self.

hunger is primal. air is a tough suck.

not everyone eats.

(my) Father has said he will not.

if you can't hear your lover, why eat?

a sizzle of chestnut-backed chickadees buzzes while Anna's
hummingbird rests on a blossomless broom branch.

replace food with emptiness, but hunger never lets you forget.

there are more than forty techniques for torture. with names like:
tucker telephone   *la parilla*   *cachots noir*

97.   USA   Chile   Rwanda

i am a still island lapped by birds. moss is a furry coat on this log,
buffed by fern fronds.

to punish.   to humiliate.   to intimidate.

my word account hungers. silent with loved ones.

feather-silent, in partial amnesia. hungry. desperate. adrift.

deny, then gulp at every offering.

can't stop the whispers, the dark drift. the wound tries avoidance.
but —

it wasn't so much, as i said, the buzzing, as the idea.

all is erasings. blade-bite. gum-rubber crumbs. a small itch.

idea of sting. not as bad as stung. but unnerving.

the speaker using ordinary speech.

bees, after all, need the nectar of the salal bud. salal is prodigious
green, leather-leafed and berried.

109.   to coerce.   to terrify.   to extract.

         is he?

poetic tongue and fibre set aside. or is it play that grips?
the difference a letter trips.

this is the poem that cannot deny snow or salal.

this premise a promise.

traps.

does it promise acuity?

tropes

promiscuity?

it's not easy, with words. all speaking in accents. words attempt.
tempt.

nectar-suckers. feather shafts.

i know (my) Father well but He is a mystery.

inside each of us a secret. hidden earmarks and coverts. flashes
seen. taking off. alighting.

because his eyes gleam and gaze into you.

you know by now of my regard for (my) Father, and that i seek
birds, their habitats, identities.

do you? do i?

125.   traits challenge. backyard sparrow snapped in the trap. caught in
the mouse war.

flipping through guide books. forgetting to look in the need to
name. hunting like mad through glossary, index. cannot live a day
without taxonomy.

the pattern of, clue to, the veiled, greater scheme.

speech can blind the speaker. words shrink from view. syllables
break on the ear's rim. they flee our longing, leave unease in
their wake.

don't leave me, in Dad's diction. in his mouth. as if through a
hollow.

well-deep. farewell-deep.

Saffron, a crescent carved into farm field at the edge of Toronto
in 1961.

deep, unparsable desolation. deeper than disappointment. His
body cowering to the wall. fending. loss. severed dream.
a bent way.

crocus sativus likely came from the orient. it was used by
Cleopatra, was known to Greeks and Romans, and appears in the
song of Solomon.

the crush. circling in obsession. the pressure. wish for control.

hangover. withdrawal. letter-quiver.

torture is used today in many countries. even in respectable
democracies. like yours. or is condoned by silence.

hovering ideas. high hopes, blown sky-high. shattering of hope.
toxins taken in a blink. allergen-bite. anaphylaxis. air is a
tough suck.

my eyes blink to a cathedral of fir and cedar.

to left the fallen mother-trunk. ahead the sunbathed meadow.

anguish is primal, loss-adorned.

danger game. strokes and whorls and spars that never cease to
swirl me.

letter-forest. ecology is not the issue. or is it? a way to avoid
futility. guzzling directories, rumpled lists.

disappointment is to bemoan obsessive about anything else.

144. or reach for the serotonin re-uptake inhibitor. the mystery of
photosynthesis.

else is what you do not have.

falls from the lips of the speaker. wordshorn-one. words awash,
wash up eventually to lap at edges. stroking lips away.

tangents. we tangent, me and my other. that word from grade ten
geometry.

thousands and thousands have been tortured.

propositions too. no ability to say no. or stop making them.

bald eagle overhead. i am always in flight, wanting to taste
everything but the allergen.

to settle rarely. words let me love and leave 'em. words, alas, have
other mouths.

teardrop. oar. torpedo.

a stalk of oatgrass springs free of a clutch of salal in berry. white
topsy-turvy teardrop-fat buttons belly out beneath shiny leaves. i
think deer eat them, but i'm no authority.

the chair will be willed to me.

first thought *snow-drops*. later they turn blue, the berries. i like
that — play of colour.

and alphabet. its logical illogic.

narcissism of the first person pronoun. engage the i-am bit
odometer.

for example, *the five techniques*: food deprivation, hooding, sleep
deprivation, forced standing, noise bombardment.

some clutch convention for control.

or strangers.

161.   an injection to fix. or to induce pain, contortions.

wallets disappoint, empty or lost. everything at risk.

toxins seek Evelyn's body's pockets as a market of exchange. deals
or no, loss calls.

word is an offer i can't refuse. easy, wanting. propositioned by
even a letter, i fall. cast off garb and notions of escape.

165.   a fly on the page. arriving, the first ferry of the day. few people
on deck. those not complacent or weary. can't hear them over
wavewash.

Evelyn on intravenous support. word ions lurking beneath any report, subcutaneous inject-text.

hear thrumming. and buzzing translucent wings. a black glyph surrounded by white.

flat black clouds menace the mainland forty kilometres away. sun needles my bare arms.

winged glyph returns, alights above the letter *d*.

170.   the tidal race through the pass is obviously complex, turns and turns on itself. its currents chiaroscuroed by the rising sun reflecting off riplets and pulls.

in a wave of memory (my) son-king crowns from his first sea into air. fish are sucked in the watery draw. boats capsize, sailors go down.

because i am awed and am two lives now.

what if that *d* were the last remaining letter of the last alphabet. how to speak it?

174.   correction: three lives now. (no echo of Stein intended). though leave no stone untended.

that last island surrounded by eternity.

what sounded letter will be the last to fall from my lips in slipping clutch of the glyph before i glide into tongueless white?

revision: five lives now.

because (my) son's openness aches into me.

a basset hound has limited vocabulary. his tongue hangs, he cares not. un-self-conscious of this or his short legs and drooping ears. letter *m*. crest and trough.

white sea these strokes try to fill. can't bother to come to an offered hand.

the pass is a vein between islands. among possibilities.

his bark a deep churr in his throat.

used to be a poet. writing sentences now. where is the line? drawn? feathered out.

Evelyn has stabilized. her platelets were down but they gave her a transfusion of normal blood. market of exchange.

third morning ferry, *of Nanaimo*, draws through the pass. queens in procession. regardless. even a boat is named.

i have nothing of sea, of self, to say with authority.

that sparrow, white-crowned, many words later, singing from the same branch. and days.

no point waiting. or resisting.

its song. a walking stick may balance. a twig. or stylus. serifs hook.

whatever holds you up or gets it down. needle-song. inside each, a secret yearning seraph.

i hear a tune in my head but i'm no Tom Waits. nor his lurking brother Trouble. though distress dogs me.

words are bark. are sap. are branching, root-clutch. similes are not precise. or like themselves.

the dictionary is my chief supplier. or is it? (which came first?)

random cut. an *oxfordized high*. toward the end, at high school i was low. very low.

(my) Father, sunken into hopelessness.

196.　shriek of the broom-saw is too shrill for contemplation. an island is like that. you can only get so far before you're back.

a small paragraph.

inside each of us a mystery.

we circle.

through the clouds, sun feathers fairy-glitter on the water. shadows on the present tense. (for the lucky).

201.   Evelyn, gone.

these mornings are sacred. the miracle of photosynthesis. birdsong.

the glide of edges. approaching distance, juncture of light and tissue.

Father is an island. word-shored. in a roil of words. loss-adorned. pouring.

205.   *administrative practice of inhuman and degrading treatment.*

pontifications bridging, to the next and next. words, His gnaw and rah and rat-a-ta-tat.

wind constantly inventing the gaze.

words lap at Him, lap from Him, transgress His skin in all directions. He devours their black symbology.

209.   *the lesion of the response.*

they are His hors d'oeuvres.

the irony of any attempt.

His entree, His bran, His dessert and beverage.

words enter His eyes His ears His porous flesh. He devours them.
His being, the word. His raison d'être, the word. His risk and
resilience, the word. His hiding place in the pressure. He grasps for
their order to allay His confusion.

walking the perimeter of the electric fence, followed by yoga
practice, is relaxing, and rousing to hunger.

He rants and runs. sentences betraying Him.

wind-buffed feather in the grass.

the re-sig-nation. departure of signs from the unsaid body.

218.   left with the ashes of His phrase. *under that rock on your island,*
He said.

unsentencing.

hunger draws me, wet or feather-dry to scan the reservoir of words.

held onto in the coming apart of things.

i write, hollow-boned. rattling at his words.

the sea is steely blue and swallows at high tide.

(my) blind hand. coffee spatters on the page.

contusion.

such staining and words.

happening throughout the sounding music that pulls.

this kicking. unnatural going backward. a frog — the wound
imitates with fins — would be embarrassed.

and it's all about fish. where are they?

not a cloud in the opalescent sky. water so clear. in the shallows i
can see the bottom.

at rock bottom. nothing to see but tendrils of plants, turtleshell
stones. ribbons of light.

but i always go too far.

knees ache my confidence away.

let my legs stretch and drift. lapping waves are gradual music.
aspen a timbre of trembling, nervous golden beauty.

it is good to be here. the place of intuition. words arc and fall and
quiver in the water. a question of alignment.

i claim to be writing after music. or toward it. tentacles of desire
reaching.

the automatic opera of meadows and lakes. illusive coup d'état in
lymph nodes. nuclear plants.

because the honesty in his face demands my humility.

i have no credentials, but a twenty-five dollar license. twelve square
inches of impunity.

whipping with barbed wire.

don't even know my limit.

incidental, instrumental. incremental. disaster is everywhere.
though hides from me here.

wanted: a black wheel barrow to cart off abstraction.

possessive pronoun is an oxymoron.

net is empty.

glass cuts into the tires.

the kitten climbs into the motor.

very tight tying of the hands, often used on women and children.

pray for loved ones. 249.i. choose strawberries; 249.ii. not snack crackers.

i can't imagine the final moment. a lovely but strange day on the lake.

churches burned.

three or four *rises*, as they call them.

necessity of jargon.

shift of attention. no use pretending.

255.   whiskey-jacks, a pair, bold and persistent are paid off with crumbs
and red berries. they were luckier than we.

flicker and song drawing attention to the tall spruce. forest fire
didn't touch this lake or its surrounding hills.

the wounds of saffron.

i'm surprised by this extended form because my aim was fixed on
terse, allusive. the sentence will not let

me go on. it breaks by interruption, poly-laterality.

normality is relative.

political, social, propagandistic, manufactured. a slipknot
tightening.

they're not biting. *it has to do with the pull of the moon,* a man
says. *won't be good for eight more days.* is there magic
in numbers?

i read and read. pronouns shift. who are *you*?

there is music in Nova Scotia.

hollow airs and severity.

gun shots at Burnt Church. over sea life.

what matters? drawn butter isn't good for cholesterol count. but neither is a gun.

for coffee the French press method is good if you like it rich, almost chewy.

beating with clubs, blackjacks, rubber hoses, telephone books, whips.

are humans fish out of water? what is a fish's perception of wind?

will i ever return to verse?

for better or for.

utterly.

a break in the processual nature. how to measure?

photosynthesis occurs in green plants, seaweeds, even algae and certain bacteria.

many have written about music. notes on notes. note by note.

277.   not far away. wounds of Phnom Penh, Kent State, Tiananmen, New York, Baghdad.

what is the purest form of writing about writing?

in the poetry garage the engine is apart.

writing writing.

full. of questions. will answers empty me through the weightless ceiling of the dark?

pull of the breeze. sun's warm kiss. children can be frank.

unnerving. (my) son is a joker and a referee.

because of his smile and his honesty.

disaster, the undertone of human art.

we'll fish and we'll fish. impatient, but convinced.

tears bulb below containing surfaces. lovepain rhizomes deep in your plexus.

bloodFather, languagegriller. from your centre your self is crumbling.

Father and fathers. chefs of baked potatoes and words. flake is key.

lock plundered. home asunder. thin possibility of rebuilding. He gets moving.

small possessions padded and packed and sealed in boxes.

heart-flayed, my Father. i am doing what i can with corrugated board and tape.

forced walking on the open jagged rims of tin cans.

because his love locates my hiding place.

to hold. to fix His name to this life. Clarence Alfred. His clarity altered by caesura and altercation.

the wind constantly inventing itself.

i am the only offspring. Dad and i going it alone. together.

298.   one Wah. 'n' pretending to pretend while reworking his words into his book in my hands. bio-friction.

writing nothing is valid.

tear-bubbles are not fake in our ducts. fluids rule us.

the havoc-truth of deficit.

the chair He falls asleep in. with me nearby. again and again.

paper and binding and words.

others speak, filtering through.

305.   i have journeyed east to start His journey west, His shift from death to life. (or so i thought.) compasses whirl.

hair coming out. combing and combing, getting the part just so, then brushing out death, thinking His heart will unroot.

307.   a stone atop a fencepost.

i mark a box with words. the signified packed, sealed off.

Father and i. uncommon collaboration.

He is on a rope and knows no way of getting off.

He repacks my box-in-progress. collision.

uncomfortable corm, this anger.

313.   Wah talks of father's power. kids riddled with fatherblood, awed
by fatherpower that, in them (us), takes root.

time is a power-shifter. beware of absolutes. their tendency to fall.

life force forked to death by lymph glands. (our) bodies, the tool
for this energy. utensil for language. plague.

torturers are trained in the arts of *hood, submarino, field telephone*
and *pau de arara*, to name just a few.

and as the toll takes itself and His-self and (your)self, the tool fails
and words move on.

what reason for the stone?

the lake a gray-blue dish rimmed green and gold and topped with
huge bulbous clouds. heaven-torch. or mounds of orange gelati.

neoprened, belly-boating, i'm trolling the lake called Sealey.

the spin, these days, of words.

no evidence in sight, but a reason to believe in fish.

a novice finning the edge.

the accordion was the instrument Pauline Oliveros took up at age ten or eleven.

who invented this? a front-kicking, back-drifting tube i'm seated in, sealed, self-propelled, unreeling line. to fool the fish. or to imagine fish near the caddis flies where the bank drops off.

in another place, the world seemed to be a sidewalk.

clicking reel. who's fooled? lured.

body is a tempted tongue slipping easily toward aspen shimmer. toward the middle of the lake. its wind-blast and hard waves.

piercing fear. knee-joint ligament a snapping rubber band.

330.   between sunrise and sunset *i am only wound and mud.*

the lake a huge jaw biting my knee.

332.   newspaper report of an Iraqi soldier dangling in a net hung from a fork-lift. blasting wind that fights my return to the narrow hills.

tourist in the pressured surround. strange water walking surface bug.

(my) filter, (my) failure.

hatchings may be finished for the season. what kind of bug to imitate at the end of the line.

at the end of (my) time?

fish are canny or too lazy to agitate the hook.

over there, sunlight impales on a rampike. blackened back five years in a forest inferno. charred spikes, ankle-brushed now with gold and auburn bush.

thunderrumble. i'm green and tawny. green and calling on auto-hypnosis to calm. green with the sudden fear i won't get back.

photosynthesis provides the basic energy source for all organisms.

three guys. hundreds of trout. hundreds of reasons to believe in fish.

pain made intense by panic. torch flickers. imagine the
burning hills.

whole worlds aflame.

barking above, the snow geese. a white escape toward the gather
of darkening clouds.

gelati melted and slumped in the bowl.

i've made it to the reed-bed, skirting shore. assured, calmer now.

house of mud and sticks. peer for the hidden entrance. no bucky
rodents surface to defend. no encounter with the wild. but
the wind.

348.   *reason to believe*. Tim Hardin sang this beautifully in '67 or '68, at
a cafe on Yorkville when i was young and he was still alive. he was
jumpy and junked and disjunctive.

burning the soles of the feet. burning of the sex organs.

the vibrato of reeds.

nary a fish-jump here. memories rise and get away. can't go back.
a long way to the dock. safe in a belly-boat, but lightning
could strike.

colours vanish in the duskening.

horror continues at distance.

people get rich in the strangest ways.

there is reason to doubt.

because his searching fingers turn music in me.

a sentence is a contrivance. what of a phrase?

the purity of the phoneme. lightning would vaporize my blood.

on a thin line. fish-wishing.

human intelligence, so capable. the cliché of thought.

imagine a narrow hill.

the astonishing shimmer of birch and aspen leaves in the fall.

knowing, uncertain of what's to come.

364. *the poem is prayer,* says Beckett. prays to?

itself? other?

raise one, or other, above?

the destruct of hierarchy.

hired poet, here. at work. word-digger. archaeologist in logos' locus. these fat white morning benedictions. so much can be made of snow.

logologist?

370. i continue to read the snows of Celan, their anguish.

kneeling, devout vocalizer.

i have no right to my innocent snow, or the word *anguish*.

if the fisherman, in the spring, sees two magpies, it means good weather and good fishing.

falling.

the scrape and scape of (his) snow. i have little right to this white
page to imagine in. after his snow-pocked crystallinity, my crude
and pampered words, too easily cast.

but, this snow.

particles curtain the end and part to beginnings.

snow fluffs up railings (not rant, but parapet, prop).

eyes too-easily-tricked, angled with get-go, the pleasured surround.

a blade will let me lean over the ice. into the snow. and
snows-to-come glinting in (our) air.

snow-crystal, ash-rind, firefly. glimpsed in our

falling.

blossomless. evocative absence.

384.   ligature : obbligato

the Futurist said *the cost of everything will increase dramatically.*
Father, about to retire, looked in the mirror, went back to work for
five more years.

le petit déjeuner for a Zairian prisoner in 1982 — drinking his own urine.

"Don't think those weren't the longest years of my life. Thinking every day where else I could be."

i can imagine.

389.

"Good thing though. I'm better off now."

even now after so much loss. after withering around death. after spin and fall, crashing face-first to the sidewalk.

392.   the Futurist wrote: *Except in struggle, there is no more beauty.* and also: *Time and Space died yesterday.*

"Ever since I banged my face and the side of my head, I don't hear well."

"I noticed."

"Eh?"

Rilke speaks of the open gaze of the animal or child. or lovers at first blush. pure space fallen into.

le déjeuner — beating on the shoulders.

rose of saffron.

the way, blizzard-blind, one drops then curls into oneself. cold becomes a warm blanket.

the shape of farewell. coil of back. black bead of blood. black pearl of tear.

He was resisting, working against the flutter and gleam, to find the oblivion He thought desired Him.

in a curl one begins.

the uncoil of be.

we blush and are made aware. thus loss and beginning of blind good-bye.

uncoil : recoil.

apart? order pot. rodeo.

continual wind and rewind toward beginning. our circle complete, is imperfection. once complete. once.

i'm going to live to be one hundred and thirty
(my) son says, lucky stones and jackpots in his pockets.

bruise at the eyebrow   scab on the shin
rip in the ligament   stitches at the wrist
weal on the cheekbone   stab in the groin.

talisman scars.

beatings with shovels, planks, gun barrels, lamp cords, rat-filled
sacks.

*"I think of a lot of things to tell somebody or you. Then when I'm
here I don't remember them."*

we held back. each holding our own bundle became a family of
islands. stranded mouths. anchored arms. eyes searching,
longing across.

the wave of the poem falls on one beach. on a beached one. once,
and again, and again, and against.

the family poem is dysfunctional.

416.   Robert Kroetsch may think, (for we can't be sure of the speaker),
        that *poems are a longing for an end* or are a sailing *brick*.

        because his dancing legs flow into me with motion's vivacity.

        i think they are longing. but each for a different other. the brick
        will come later.

(perhaps when something solid is needed in the figurative dark)

words press into the surround. *approach embedded in the poem.*
always an approach. what word pressures your drum? *only*
approach. when is the beat your own?

toward a shadow.

now it seems that parts of Him are missing. they are parts of me.

rhyme and rhythm of the mirror.

shed of the passions of golf, and of boyish tenderness with His
wife (who's been taken) He is a man of drastic action, but He is
lessening, hemmed by losses and fears.

and the light

He is the sum of years practicing subtraction.

what face cements onto your bones?

428.   perhaps this is the way . . . (about His head the newspaper flutters
as it always has) . . . He begins to leave.

photo. synthesis. light. composition. building. with. Light.

it is embedded in. as they crack.

striving for disintentional sprawl.

because he is himself as i've known him since before his first breath. we've grown and are growing. up, and together.

de-composition.

misread *matters* as *mattress*.

but not compost.

for example, the *black slave* — an electrical apparatus that pushes into the anus a hot metal skewer.

a screened window open to the world closed to the room He reclines in.

nor compote, for that matter.

439.   *Our goal is to drown you out.*

we leave Him here for now. in His inclination. He has many words to read before He sleeps.

words are a dream i cannot sleep into.

fear of disease and accident distracts.

the confessional poem is a mannequin.

confection.

rod trap. prate. oreo.

moss and sage greening in the soil at our feet.

the wound is a confession.

everywhere the vampires are in charge. i am useless flipping pages.

the poem opens like a chocolate wrapper and is swallowed whole.
without a second thought.

without a second thought. without a second to spare. i waste.

tongue-strung.

He is always telling (my) son to be careful. He was always careful with His hair, the shine on (His) shoes, with (His) money. He was careful with emotion, hoarded even from Him/self.

poems hoard their best lines. the cupboard locked.

poets dream, if blessed, through their ears.

so many exhaustions. so many typographies misshapen, misspoken.

misplaced. up and down the fonts. frontal. fontanelle. (the poem may seep here before the closing).

457. one quarter of a son's year slipping by on the way to lucky 7. one twelfth of an equinox. tilt and arc of seasons. (look back to 7; to 74.)

quarterly product race.

umbrella plant waits by the wintry window for return to shiver-free tropics.

last night sleep was a wobble with pressure.

he might sing his way in, though off-key. uncharted.

randomness has its limitations, i imagine . . . well, I can't be sure.

guess. gesture. grope. time aplenty. time absenting. a whiff. a wish.
a tongue curling on a snowflake.

whispers.

sleep off uncertainty (if i could). sweep it away. sway. weep.

the familiar may be a grove. a beach, a rock, a river. or that
misplaced word. offer a bauble to call it back.

wheeler-dealers, after treasures in a bottle. magpie scavengers, we
squeeze fat necks into the narrow orifice. stealer, stuck.

m-a-a-a-ag spieler.

words reel in and out. fly-fishing for airy diction.

word hoard. scritch of pencil point, rounding and flattening.
fuzzying at edges. stacks of font savoured, slathered over.
letter-litter.

frosting smatters us as the mercury drops. we're in for it but so far
so good.

says who? this matter, of opinion.

no movement. no collision-spur, no spawn. fin or feather,
(fluttering invocation) such an unrefined mix of plotting font. no
beauty here. or economic use. the whole thing better left unsaid.

spongy-lettered hand-job.

pOet O-T-L. *Oh give me a break. Oats and beans and barley grOw. O give me a hOme.*

the chair He scowled in. His fortress-chair.

lizards were found in their living-room eating their owner. seems they were hungry. lacking respect for authority, death.

lizard logic hard to figure. the reptilian brain. lives in each of us deep in the stem. or is it cortex?

before knowledge.

today, bad weather. don your gortex brain.

and speaking of liz-ards and time — no insult intended
— Liz Taylor was a beauty in hers. though this piece lacks her compelling, voluptuous looks.

it trails off, skitters down a tube. some days are like that — a scaly gnawing nuisance.

483.   and speaking of Liz, before he knew her, *Oh* sang a young Michael JacksOn *Give me One mOre chance.*

the place sought. sough of words sounding you in. in-ness. raw-ness. octaves haunting in to you.

an avalanche of snow slides down a windshield. a blind eye opening.

another music calls but you hear it not. faulty music?

old grandpa has a few creaks in the bones, says (my) boy with a laugh, walking with stiff-hipped imitation, and fluid with empathy.

faulty hearing?

in the north of Italy and the south of Switzerland saffron is essential in the preparation of risotto.

forget order, comprehension.

lifting women by the hair.

492.   speak toward *the fourth part of utopia,* says Lisa Robertson, *suppressed by the existent horizon.*

if this is polyphonic, is it polymorphous?

the kiss of a leather sole across the dusted hardwood.

slither and glide of fibreglass on a crystal bed.

496.   her ecstatic hips grinding beneath me on the cotton sheets.

because his bony shoulders bear a state of grace.

the sun is inaudible, and though fading, is all afternoon.

what is the word for forget?

what is the shape of abandoned?

opera. port. toreador.

what is the notness of intention?

this is the poem that can leap the seasons.

plants making glucose.

the poet writes a manifesto: IN WHICH the poet ATTEMPTS TO
UNDERSTAND WHAT he IS DOING.

the poem is a gleaming object, scarred and buried under wreckage.

a thing too beautiful may cross the line, tripping the wound toward terror.

because his skin is terrifying.

509.   ears, fingers, toes, or genitals, alligator-clipped to the live shock-wire. used by Americans, this was called the *field* or *Tucker telephone*.

bare the wires. turn the crank.

between lift. and light. *ligament, ligate, ligature.*

the binding slur between notes invisible in the sounding the song made possible.

to move outside the notion of the poem as a temporal motif. to move outside the notion of moving on from one to the next. to be hesitant and sinuous.

quiet articulation of the books that cluster.

fevered with the absent poem's heat.

striving is not arriving.

back to that known map of the old poems, their comfortable chair.

perhaps i am the afterlife of kingfisher, hovering, regurgitating to build my nest.

the unassuming poem erases itself but leaves a trace.

perhaps (if you are reading).

are you?

you are considering the stability of the structure of random twigs and threads.

my make-do dream.

524. and in Sweden saffron bread is traditionally baked on the day of St. Lucile.

i don't mean this as adequate. the verbs are active.

that fallen nest, small and brown, but glinting, found by (my) son.

(why write of the poem, in the poem?)

a weave of grass and string. strands of acetate. and threads of silver garland. cupped in a boy's tender hand, discovering.

can never write the poem intended.

i'd flown to His side to try to coax Him back from oblivion. He said, *I've really buggered things up this time, haven't I?*

so out with intention.

(even this is intention).

word asunderer.

What do you mean? i said
Just look. You'll know what I mean.

poet, plunderer.

cold-snap that snaps and snaps.

long lines to wrap and warm your neck.

but tongue's pulled out from under you.

perhaps it is simply fear you will become the one who never arrives. wanderer with no story, no aboutness. you will abrade space with absence. an invisible wound.

for some it is chocolate. for others a cow. or a whip.

you have read that the wind speaks in a different timbre through
each species of tree.

542.   says Lisa Robertson *if we abandon a pronoun an argument
is lost.*

spruce sing the blues.

the voice of a child is capable and clear.

a dog is not diminished by wanting to be human. to meet another
kind in its skin is reverence. unblemished rapture.

i have not understood suicide.

(side beyond words).

until now. ride into night.

549.   some live in Lispector's *light of the axe.*

or its falling shadow, soothing shadow, that blanks the
hollowing gnaw.

the departed slices his pain back into the world through the veins
of beloveds.

leg or thumb screw, vice-like implement fixed to a limb or digit and
turned tighter to squeeze. and tighter.

553.   Saffron was the crescent i lived on in my late teens, and there
remained the family home, for twenty-five years.

to escape, to escape.

555.   love disguises itself with feathers and tin, invites you and you
plunge and in heat and reflection you don't hear the *axe's hiss*.

the word *love* is huge and puny. a thousand-strand coil. complex
as deoxyribonucleic acid.

could say it was torrent, tearing, torment, shook me through the
jaws of the beast.

but won't.

the confessional poem is a mannequin dressed for display. it bends,
undressing in a window.

we are borrowed from our stories.

i enter indebted, a beggar.

the wound understands *risk* and *loss*.

order. waiting for orders, someone to command. the man, waiting for words. the boy, waiting. near the net for a pass.

(because his life reveals the unpredictable certainty of death).

poem waiting, refusing. poet, waiting, refusing order. words waiting, refusing.

the dream takes place on the forking road.

terra raw.

at the fork of frozen intention we are halved.

tear roar.

and the pass never comes.

a child, stuffed in a sack with a feral cat, in front of bound parents.

wound stumbles in a direction of questions. bells tolling behind. singing of a skin left back there.

prickly but soft frost clings to pine-needles in spite of the wind.
wound is surprised that the wind is not colder. stops,
closes eyes, waits.

everything crushes but the wound is still standing.

so much dwelling in the mouth. tooth cracks. leaves a gaping
channel for. misspoken words. and food that will enter. mouth is
home. spilling forth.

we are our own doppelgangers.

(my) Father arrives but can't explain how He got lost, or got here.
just by walking.

destiny's density.

579.   spring whispering its name from a reddening stalk. from a broken
ice ledge. from the warm edges of a gauzy sun.

at the edge of thought begins dissociation. and finding.

a magpie on a wire is a galoot wearing a tattered, yet striking
tuxedo. a good act.

it's about waiting. but words want to fill.

patience is an aid.

wanting to discover the right words about wanting.

denial of the pronoun, of the self in any form is an impossible twist.

author as posed otherity.

writing spring with the ghost hand of winter.

your skin is a drawn webbed mesh stretched across razored accusations that demand another you.

a wound to the head. blood trickling down the nape.

590. the babe wears a fake zebra-skin coat over a plastic zebra gown off-shoulder, sloping dangerously over her left breast. this is what the poem wants to be. an articulated philosophy of stripes and jags, the provocation of a tossed hip, the bud of a nipple rising to the eye.

earlier tonight the poem sat with its Father who spoke of pushing up daisies. Father who's returned to single digit numbers though still loves the pluses (pulses) and minuses of the stock exchange.

this line in an ocean of words in a bowl whose rim is never reached.

the poem has a pointy chin, but worries about its fat cheeks.

the poem is an ice-cream cone.

fluttertongue: air uttered   up from the gut, from lungs   longing.

thinking: th' inking of the poem.

shoulder aches in the hands of the lovely physiotherapist. pain can
have its reward.

snowfall so slight it's almost a lie.

how much ache will you bear for beauty?

this is not the poem you were looking for.

all verse is of the wound.

this is the poem you were not looking for.

heart-flayed, (your) Father.

ice-slick refuses passage. refuses (your) destination. refuses
the poem.

poem attempts to hold precipitates in suspension.

the pronoun can be too proud. the possessive pronoun is a wound.

poem is a suspension bridge.

love or grudge. love or scorekeeping.

we mistake the signs.

the love poem has a headache.

strappado, known as *the corda* or *cola*. the victim's hands tied
behind the back. a rope through a pulley or over a beam is lashed
to his bound wrists. then by the wrists, he's hoisted into the air,
hung there. suddenly he's dropped, jerks to a stop above
the ground.

things go better with.

as spring breaks, the juniper berries seem to plump themselves blue
from winter gray. or is this assumption?

614.   chickadees pluck them, then fly up from the low bush to the tree
branch where they hold a berry with their toes and beak-poke to
get the soft meal.

back and forth. back and forth. flying and eating like mad.

survival.

what does *like mad* mean?

now's everywhere. jerks us to a stop. or not.

breathing is all we have.

now sudden snow. sight of white. flurries blurring the eyes of the
whiteness witness.

what *takes our breath away* gives reason to go on.

news is a topical wound.

the poem, a construction of breath.

the nurse pretended to take my pulse, but was really counting
breaths. *you'd speed up,* she said, *if you knew.* the lungs apparently
have consciousness.

because his demand for explanation weakens my confidence
in words.

your breathing is fine, she said.

i was worried about my heart.

as if i was somebody else in the hospital bed. an *other*, not in the philosophical sense.

hold the poem's wrist.

in the thick darkening, blacker than blood, blacker than eyes that no longer see. light may follow.

thirty years ago. *He* that resembles *i* is building it. exposed brick and billowing room. someone unfamiliar also there, offering encouragement. a window, open, high over a glittering river, chorusing with stone songs. *He-i*, too, becomes a stranger. but the dream is mine.

breath takes you there. up the high road, skirting the ice.

in the snow, fresh weasel tracks. behind, from the river, the constant wonky-honk of geese.

everything a living trace that pulls against painful resistance in your chest. at any second.

635.   lost in thought. scrunch, rustle, up-flutter partridge. startles the daylights. out of you. out of brush. off through trees. eyes about. to see. can't be sure. neither is the bird. and later, pictures, flipping pages to name. sureness gone. but in the ear. a beating wing.

beating heart. *you look good,* he says. *i look better than i am,* i reply.

inside where he can't see.

the wound sits in a chair and weeps over a broken heart.

later i walk the treadmill but can't go on. can't explain
looking good.

640.   nitro under tongue. diltiazem washed down with breakfast. aspirin
every day. blockage. body defeating itself.

in Spain saffron is an indispensable ingredient in such famous
dishes as paella, fabada, fideua, or pote gallego.

fobbed galley poet.

the body begins as a poem as a wound.

how final is any moment?

645.   the Queen Mother dies just as March ends. (my) Uncle Joe dies the
next day, one before April fool's. same day as (my) friend's father-
in-law. another friend a week later. all dead, as the dead of winter,
clutching hard.

winter is pried away by spring. but not without its claim.

ascension day. a bitter wind. two bald eagles spiralling over the
field, mocking our kite's nose-dive into snow-crusted earth.

how to write the jolt-poem.

the chair, sulked in.

son horizon.

tumbling from the lips, the knowing before knowing.

is it possible that language is exhausted?

the poem can/will never be the same.

i don't know.

dear toe, prod torpor.

656.   triftazin. stelazine. haloperidole. chlorpromazine. trifluoroperazine.

Think of an artery as a donut. We've been paying a lot of attention to the hole. Now we're looking at the donut itself.

up-roar.

659.   poor choice for metaphor. will raise your LDL.

what pastry is the poem?

pockets erupt sending fragments into the blood stream.

the body is a confection bomb.

663.   the spirit of the saint-maker, of Orm, Ein, Alwart. as darkness
settles a dusty mauve-gray at the edge of the seeable, that friend,
always young, comes.

now the poetry at the edge of the future.

fear of unidentified sounds.

you look up often since, overhead, to the roar in the sky or the
high glass.

what words can describe the pall?

constancy of blood and nectar.

one slips in, enters in the middle:

that young moose fallen in the stream.

one takes up or lays down rhythms says Spinoza via Deleuze.

your rhythm is a vice-grip around your chest.

all these tests and medications.

this spring everything is reluctant. pelicans huddled in snow. lilac clutching back its buds.

nitroglycerine pushing open the blood vessels.

crocuses crowning, get pelted, lost under snow.

677.   in a later season your heart might look like a cotton burdock.

678.   or pinedrop.

slitting the nose.

bold purple spiky burdock.

pinedrop's urn-shaped cream-brown flowers on a blood-red stem in July.

two year old moose, her loping stride brought down by parasites.

jaw and eyeball stripped to blood-drenched bone. chained round the neck hoisted into air.

heart as flower.

you look and look but there is no form.

only motion, a relationship of velocities.

because his thin vulnerable body makes the poem possible.

and impossible.

swings above the stream, above cattail, death camas.

slung on the John Deere gallows. then lain across the forks.

carried up, lowered to the grassy plain, host to pulsing visitations of coyote, magpie, crow. and the wind.

nitro, cardio, angio.

wind becomes melody. adagio.

the aspen a timbre of trembling.

695.   *listening, listening in a total way to the sound, to the quality of the sound, to be completely open to sound,* says Pauline Oliveros.

under the tongue vibration waits.

lilting, lowing, throughout the sounding music.

698.   normalcy is relative. political, social. propagandistic, manufactured. *beaten bloody with batons.*

pronoun is matter, sings with and alone.

the hybrids are coming.

through photosynthesis organisms become sugar-making factories.

702.   i treasured it. i made a gift of it to a lover. (love can make us generous). love passed. thirty years passed. a friend (who did not know my lover) offers me this gift. beyond explanation.

703.   *"there's never one mouse."*

a stem of white birch lies, dying on the black of the forest path. a stark bone, crumbling, moving backward in time, and forward.

and now, the poetry of falling.

rub the blackness in until it pales.

a cup rattles in its saucer as he writes.

the poem visited and revisited by moths. their clumsy flutter and dusting. this one on his back flicking and flicking his wings, and turning in helpless circles.

709.   John Cage said *Our poetry is now the realization that we possess nothing.*

yet we fence.

this morning, like (his) Father, the wound wrestles with a plastic bag, arranging things in it. a cup, a bowl, glasses, a book. in the carry everything is scrambled. even the mind. in the crook'd arm, the ache of possession.

wound's rhythm is interrupted.

eagle, lost in the flare of the sun.

"I was just following orders."

people falling.

"I'm going to get a tattoo in each armpit. Daisies."

(my) Father's legs running out from under him His hands clutching bags torso lurching ahead of legs leaning to catch up torpedoing arcing down head first face bashes the sidewalk.

from the sky.

the self-possessive pronoun may be whole. here a puzzle, there a wobble.

battered. bloody. stitched. bruised.

forced listening to incessant loud noise.

the death of a loved one is a form of torture.

after Evelyn died, His world in pieces that wouldn't fit.

the wound seeks flatness. numbing monotony.

paintings — say, a wall of Rothko's dusky crimson, or the gray meditations of Agnes Martin.

one tortures (oneself) with the disappearance of the possessive pronoun.

in these spaces of unity and uninterruptedness, peace can be found, and all that surrounds takes meaning, fresh and pure.

crushing knuckles and testicles with pliers.

such awareness is brief. you must keep returning to the field.

because his translucent skin reveals my artifice.

it takes a long time to understand.

pocked rock massaged at its tips by soft insistent waves.

733.   a ship drifts to a dot then disappears inside itself.

a log pushed against a rock by the incoming tide longs for the forest.

uncertainty directs the wound disguised as a pen.

the cliff drops you into space.

poets dance on the rims of our ears.

eagle swoops over the edge, down, then up to a height that makes the stomach churn.

trees in their blind knowing.

the wound is a grasper. the wound in quest of relief, release.

because of scrawny muscles flexed in his seven-year-old shirtless torso as he sits on the piano bench.

listening with your cells.

foxglove should be called *thimble-glove*

or *nodding bell*

or *mouse party-hat.*

yesterday so vivid. or was it the day before? a moment ago?

piercing the tongue. cutting out the tongue.

in shade is misunderstood as

insane

a voice is torn to a whisper.

a moth is wild with ecstasy at the lantern and the page.

rattling in the glass.

Blaser should appear here with all his visions of the whacky brown-dusted winged ones.

pain is a warning. no intention but escape.

755.   a body arches in *setu banda sarvagasana*. opening.

there is a time for silence that words ignore.

757.   the blinds are up. fruits of light crane toward your page.

unspeaking Father creates a syntax of evasion.

in the softening and stretch the wound yields.

scrambling over swirls and scrapes and bones of rock. sun beats, heating this spine that stretches into salty waters to let lips taste the ocean's kiss.

the beadwork of words to trade in the marketplace.

because of the unbleared beam of his brown bright eyes.

rock. its speechless tale.

764.   the moth's *habit of light*

falanga. beating the soles of the feet. there is no name for pounding tacks into the foots' flesh. the permanent results: difficulty walking, scars that never disappear.

newsprint disguise. newsprint mothing around his head.

the herb of the sun — saffron.

blue jay jack-hammers the sunflower head. in another poem. leaves turning crisp and wan.

wound wound into every word.

how do i tell this is verse?

771.   *Once available knowledge confronts inexplicable phenomena the time has come for another breakthrough,* wrote Richard Schechner in 1981.

a lump appears at the back of my knee.

the chair, the only place He could find comfort.

774.   on the same day reading of torture. the beating, by Israeli soldiers in the Nahal Brigade, that broke bones in the legs and arms of eight Palestinian men at Beita, on the West Bank on January 20, 1988.

the pressured surround is a border, a frontier. the pulsing walls of a cyst before it ruptures.

stoning.

how to write the poetry of the future in this future, after the falling.

glass. a lake is often compared to this.

it is the other way around.

we were on it. a pontoon boat. someone at the dark end translated the phrase as *my womb aches for you.*

a thin screen of clouds made the stars seem hazy. the moon was three-quarters full. the dark edge stabbed and stabbed the light.

like a saw cut, she said.

order is regimentation.

i heard *my wound aches for you.*

order is an arbitrary form.

so many things left behind: kettle, towel, printer, thermos. disorder at every turn.

call your Father.

keyhole, towline, prism, thesis.

feather flourish.

Father frowned.

fear of unidentified sounds.

a swelling from the knee to the ankle can occur for several reasons.

you have been sitting, bound, on the floor of a bus that lurches over rocky roads. it stops and you are led into a field. a dozen men jab you with clubs and push you to the ground. they beat you on the legs and arms. and beat and beat.

Richard Schechner is the founder-director of The Performance Group.

i thought he said *beggar's.*

a torpedo or teardrop.

it's a *baker's* cyst. ruptures, sends fluid down into the calf and ankle, swelling them. the leg becomes a clumsy log.

thought *clot.*

without the article there is one letter too few to make it perfect.

they leave you to bleed into night.

september is the month of the truth of the body. the blocked artery. the swollen leg. the tumour. the cyst. the death of Aunt Eleanor.

the letter *A.* Louis Zukofsky started there and made it a whole book.

the body reminds us of its dominion, but for the last gesture. stealing from us just as we look away.

and with it, the sack of pain.

we are penned.

806.   Barry McKinnon wrote a fine book called *the the*. articles are
swelling, are taking over, look back at 801, for example.

807.   white and tawny, an undulating ripple down the slope toward the
highway. as the car approaches, the wave of pronghorns hesitates,
skitters like my Father's jittery hands, turns back and bounds
into the field, buffed pink with dawn's breaking, just as, from the
recording, the voice, Paul Celan's voice, slows to ending. leaving in
the air the now-famous ache of his goldashen lines.

a shattered book.

809.   *Jack doesn't know his own mind and is therefore a kind of poet.*

the one spared can hobble, sobbing to town for help.

skinhead. skinner. skinny. skip. skip out. skip over. skip-a-rope.
skipbomb. *skip-to-my-Lou-my darlin'.*

812.   *he knows the unbearable pressures and is therefore, also human.*

wrinkled foreheads.

your territory shrinks to the shape and size of your body. an island
of pain.

i was looking for *skirmish*. or was it *skittle*?

relativity is normal.

accessory photosynthetic pigments absorb light in the spectrums
of blue and red, and orange and yellow wavelengths. no pigments
absorb green wavelengths.

818.   *a text which was not a labyrinth would not be a text, a labyrinth*
         has its coherence, the rooms communicate with one another.

green is reflected, making plants appear so.

820.   *the 'Iraqi Manicure' (ripping out fingernails and toenails).*

light brightens me. shadows burn. this is not a metaphor.

822.   the probe bends its way through the gray, negotiating the artery's
         curve (with difficulty) inching toward the obstruction.

looking back you see no poem but a cluster of imperfections.
ahead is only absence.

inadequate provision of wheelbarrows and petals.

in a poem words inflate.

red and pink evoke if you have the eye.

bugged and bucking the pronoun crowd.

tofu will do. it's good for you.

the body is a site for jabbing, metering, sending tubes and fluids into its secrets, its shades of pink, russet and mauve.

the woods still. not a creature in sight. slight breath of breeze creates a lazy sway.

you could have sworn there was only one chair on the porch. now there are two. white and empty. phantoms are urging you to watch what comes from the forest. spectres, wordless, bringing you words.

Father frowned. disappeared way inside. plundered a boy's wish.

obligatory, the required recurrence.

re : currency. who? you of the

journeyings (improvisations).

the tyranny of numbers.

837.   & returns (insistences).

who's saying this?

pulling your leg.

not a bird to be seen. not a bird to be heard.

mountains. the wrinkled forehead of the earth.

otherwise thunderous rumble.

he said *you can forget sex*. he was wrong.

you want to break out, break away.

from the already. syntactic stricture. and cozy meaning.

easier said than (you know) done.

capillary carnival. the balloon puffs, the artery opens.

eros always rises. sex always rears its beautiful head. this is a metaphor. sort of.

849.   *sex has a lot to do with pink*, she says — the poet paraphrases to suit himself. can he be trusted?

850.   she does say *pink*. and wears it.

851.   *sex is beauty*, she says.

magpie lands on the eaves, thumps up the roof.

butler to the red squirrel?

today the poet is islanded in a round room. surrounded by tawny bent grasses and a circle of pine.

John Cage's *Sonatas and Interludes* are filled with space, but cohere. his name is a cell, but his music is *free*.

are you prepared for what you will make of things?

because his young voice polishes the air with its purity.

858.   listening as healing. seek Pauline Oliveros' *Prayers for a Thousand Years*.

this poem is between you and me, dear reader.

not as wall, but bridge.

now the responsibility is yours.

how are we doing?

they stitch me up. the end of the thread protrudes from my groin.

challenging habitual thought patterns? taking steps *ex tempore*.

oulipo numerology. plus seven. for no apparent reason.

866.   toecap the poetry is isocheimed in a rousing rooster. swabbed by teeming biangular graupel and a circulation of fireboxes.

Celan's is a darker snow, born of a chilling heat. he became an island. submerged. adrift.

there is a particular definition for *free* that i mean to be applied.

characterized by bounteous giving.

because music from his nimble fingers is a dance for my ears' delectation.

i want to see the Santa Claus parade in the mountains.

weaver searches for the probe that is filament.

photosynthesis occurs when energy, then electrons, pass from molecule to molecule in the cells of the leaves of a plant. but it is much more complex than this.

874. Santa arrives in a white carriage, pulled by a brown horse.

clitorectomy. binding the feet.

poetry is not science.

could it have been an antlerless deer?

typed *Satan* for *Santa*.

my lover is absent here.

startled me, on the path just three feet from where i passed. gray. lying in the grass, that deer stared right back without moving.

nor silence.

i smiled at this gift, moved off to disturb her no further. she stayed still, but stayed with me this far.

it was not a smile. it was a form of ecstasy.

humans and animals cannot produce glucose on their own. they rely on plants to do it for them.

but there may be poetry in silence.

the rich paucity of twenty-six herbs and stones to trace it all.

two dancers. dancing on rocks.

cachots noir — a light-starved pitch-black cell.

and earlier, their bodies as alphabet. the language of the speech-thwarted body. stutter of idea. wrench of the word's corporeality.

the static of poetry.

danceless syllables struggling to their metre.

grapple and groan to urge the rock vivacious.

can absence be *here*.

clack-clack-a-lack. rock-speak. *shchshchshchshch*. rock rustle.

leaves me speechless.
(just kidding).

in art i queue late.

897.   *the sightless realm where darkness is awake upon the dark.*

it is easy at first to confuse the singing of frogs in the distant slough
with the rolling warble of sandhill cranes high overhead.

899.   let yourself go giggly. let'rrip. letter *ipsissima verba*. speak, lissome,
for heaven's sake, and sip slowly careful of its *rising* potency.

as in : with sushi.

perhaps even with the compositions of Philip Glass.

i could have said *mounting*, and considered it sexual and
topographic titillation.

tintinnabulation.

torn (seems from air) but from vein-seams.

these damn aimless lines.

for the critics to flick if they bother.

907.   *recently ways to combat people by the nation have indeed been in.*

of the absent lover, who rustles just under the sheets in
torrid memory.

jingled into the ritual light. sun beaming over sulphur mountain.
spirits lifting at approach.

Father leans back in (His) stuffed lifelong companion-chair and
says *I don't want anything to do with Christmas.*

too far back to lift. too far black.

straight-stiff-trunked pine trees have turned black through
moments of distracted gaze, to dark relief against the fading
sky's light. you sit in a bowl whose steep edges are the mountains
sheltering the trees sheltering your round cabin sheltering you,
sheltering an idea of trees and sky.

there are tens of thousands of cells in a single leaf.

two dancers. dancing on rocks. caressed and caressing rocks that begin to speak through the body.

grass and moss cushion my feet. here a stump, there a rock, a bruise. and in the constancy of my beloved i discover the truth of old abandonment, betrayal.

you run up and run up the steep sides of the poem. the poem, a bowl you can't hold in your attention, for one tiny point on the lip is what holds your aim. you run up. all other points in the surround vanish from view as you run. and slip and tumble back to the bottom's even-ing. you run up, fall back. nothing now for release but the run of eyes and ears aloft. at the edges, through shadows, still a trace of light, a faint call.

as you run words kick from your heels.

inner tickle, let.

what is the realist poem? the reality poem?

aped parrot. rotor ode.

the chair that is the seat of a wound.

922.   afterward they put the hammer weight of a stone (brick?) on my groin to keep the artery closed. one closing, one opening. Kroetsch's notes with me off and on through the field of day and deep into 3 a.m. night. *the floodgate was open, the dam no longer a dam.*

old forms implode.

a breaking shore.

a short arcing street that curved at one end. this was where a
bending began.

pica pica. black-billed magpie is a common bird in western North
America, and also in the southern hemisphere, including Cyprus.
though well-dressed, it has a rather bad reputation, based on
superstition and undeserved tales.

in creeping gray of late afternoon, just after the wound rises from
savasana, a gray buck ambles down the slope, noses the grass, and
lies, his strong back turned to the gaze, his flexing back,
breath-gentle, and perked beneath nine-point antlers, his
radar ears twitching, as he settles to his own repose.

accordion-drone-pulse.

sonar reasoning.

a crumbling sky.

page a deaf instrument : accordingly prone to

what fret?

this and that pull.

a shadow across the pale dry meadow makes you look up.

the poem, crowded out. the round-room-wound must be aspirated.

after long sitting in His chair, the blood pressure drops. on getting up quickly, it shoots up, blood rushing to the brain. the dizzy surround.

naming as certitude. name, a lock. names can surprise. titles fall or change. this switch.

switch makes the ears ring.

        how   to

    open   the

           ear.

940.   (my) son can't wait to get painting the kitchen. tinting his way into the poem. his eager hands anticipate. his voice brushes colours in my ear.

blood-song.

pica pica. like the one about having the devil's blood on its tongue.

i could use some now — sake from heaven.

kneeling with a stick behind the knees, while the torturer stands on the victim's thighs.

words fluttering at the end of clumsy fingers.

across the sculpted rims that separate.

shifting to avoid rocks and inevitable fall.

the accordion wailing in some ethereal place way out there in the wound's sensorium.

word dream:

| verre | = | glass | = | verse |
| verse | / | rêve | / | reverse |

gulls a-riot on the river.

the pronoun is a lodger.

finger bones clatter on gun barrels.

smooth and sculpted rock, shape of sea's desire.

doubt directs the self disguised as a pen.

a shiny black ant crawls along a pale thigh through hairs that must seem a forest.

the wound is a grasper.

957.   Levinas seems almost incomprehensible, though he might say
— the wound paraphrases — *that thought is itself the meaning of being.* (or not). what am i revealing?

eagle perched on the jagged bare branch has a shiny yellow beak. in his eye, a penetrating glint.

towering fir trees, stately in their scissoring sway, audacious in their garb.

flying capes, trailing trains, upswept hair.

reach, reach, at cliff-edge, for the plunge of words.

962.   *I knock on the glass to hear a sound.*

pink, orgasmic in the sun, ecstatic faces of campion.

964.   at the brow of descent, leaning into battering wind, a devil-gust swarms me, toppling my tin-packer hat, stealing its white feather — feather a gift from (my) five year old son — sailing it across the blasted wheat field, where it disappears, lost among the tawny bending stalks.

depriving a victim of the use of a toilet.

gophers are the squirrels of the prairies. (not to be confused with the squirrels called squirrels). the gopher and the magpie suffer slights.

nonetheless they are pleased not to be rats.

and every morning He bends to put Evelyn's fuzzy black and white slippers on his own feet.

disarray : an unfamiliar harmony.

might have been an eagle moving swiftly above the trees.

971.   Cage's 1967 electronic chess-game-generated indeterminate sonic
       show. for hours and hours. listening, i waited for *something*
       to happen. thirty-five years later, still learning the un-waiting
       listening.

cultivated saffron was introduced to Spain from Persia after the
10th century. today Spain produces the highest quality saffron
spice.

happening is.

poetry withers, exhausted on the clutching vine.

975.   a computer can not only draw, but can plant and grow fractal
       trees, can create a landscape.

bush and moss cushion her soar. her ecstatic hips slither and grind.

977.   a stump, a rock. the forking of attention. pau de arara.

how low, the hollow.

trees in their blind knowing.

writing backward.

981.   all you supply will be reclaimed, recycled.

so many songs sailing on the slur sliding between the sought notes, invisibly, in night's dark directions.

the poem is the Father you are always seeking while throwing obstacles in (your) own path.

pica pica. known, for example, as a scavenger.

the wound fights the poetry of silence.

the oxygen we breathe is the oxygen released during photosynthesis.

987.   *process : notion about which the researches cluster.*

disbelieve unfledged harpsichord.

that tree is your blood-sister, your blood-brother.

forced to drink from a toilet.

make the poem a hammer ringing.

the story of the Father breaks down in the weeping chair.

sublime : terror.

magpie struts along a railing. parade of black and white and iridescent-green. magpie is a special delivery messenger.

anything goes : everything goes.

996.   there, by the weathered wagon (my) boy discovers a common yellowthroat, black-masked and olive-backed. soft and dead.

borne unto burial under the pink rock at the top of the hill.

so much other-becoming. battering wind. word-bluster tumbling in my head.

troop odor. rate drape.

the failed quest for syntactic rupture.

a black dog is a spring-coil bounding and bouncing at the door on your return. the letter *b*.

you walk with (your) mother on your left. ahead (your) son walks
with (his) mother. and in a time beyond (yours), (your) son's lover
and son.   echoes. eternities.

1003.   hesitate. but not now.

grass, bent, flaxen, and patches of green moss crunch underfoot
as i walk up the ridge for a better view of the round room where i
hunch behind the glass trying to forget (my)self and uncover
a word.

lichen-light.

never seen one before. cute, cat-weasel. find out later it's a marten,
martes americana. related to the ermine, skunk and mink, and is
a threatened species, even endangered in some areas. as it lopes,
browny-russet, perk-eared, along the log, i am held in awe,
reminded of my ignorance.

you are faint in a glass but wish to disappear as you disappeared to
Him. to write the poem of disappearance of the self.

the sallow shadows i chase with a match.

author gone other. automatic pilot. but the craft is ancient and
without remote control.

1010.   *any event is a fog of a million droplets.*

you are faint in the glass but the forest is strong in its song to you.
it rustles toward you. it speaks you as you are : glazed and fading
with the light. uttering.

1012.   in the rear-view mirror of description.

1013.   the poet Gerry Shikatani cooked fideua, a wonderful dish of fine
        pasta in a soupy seafood stew spiced with saffron, in my kitchen
        in Saskatoon in 1996. the dish is more typically found on the east
        coast of Spain.

        the manifesto is buried in the words' surround.

        that tree is your blood.

        Evelyn hovers around His chair. memory as torture.

        eggshell thinness of everything.

        the chair i will be unable to sit in, its dark engulfing.

1019.   or the lightless, tiny, rat-infested cell Maher Arar suffered in, in
        solitary confinement, for ten months in Syria in 2003.

        rock. its speechless tale.

        because of Emmett's arm hooked around my thigh, his head resting
        on my lap, my hand cupping his forehead.

        the forest's filigree of morning song.

        in softening and stretch the wound yields.

submarino. hooded. bound to a tilting plank. tipped head-first into water and held there.

1025. in each flower are only three stigmas, trumpet-shaped, bright red, graduating to yellow in the style.

the story of the Father drops into the hollow of abandonment. (my) body a hollow of hollows.

if fortunate, your effort will one day be found woven into the soft hanging nest of a migrating bird who has chosen this forest to incubate her eggs.

in silence, among centurion pine, the wound walks.

at a curve the trouble starts.

all along, imaginings of bear, cougar, elk. but the wound is no conjurer.

foretaste's fillet of morose sonority.

1032. afternoon's pale light blooms at the dry river bed. the mountain comes to attention. the wound names it *old man's resting place*. on the slope's profile, forehead, nose and chin, in state, aslant, dark eyes drinking the eastern sky.

the wound sees virtue in always watching for the dawn.

the percussion of silence.

plaque and blockage at the crook of the left anterior descending.

ripple, chime.

the open mother-trunk, ahead the summon of betrayal.

words can walk beside, race or slow, with music, can alter tone, but lack music's flashy dexterity.

how to show dynamics with typography.

tone or volume?

is photosynthesis a chance operation?

this is not new.

but is it better?

sun going pink through trees leaves a feeling of melancholy filigreed with hope.

trees' leaves and needles turning black with absence.

i mis-wrote *home* for *hope*.

is it all miss/writing? never at home in words.

but hoping?

1049. *a drop of water is thrown off by the stone*

1050. pencil drawings on the wall that, on closer look, transform to steel wool. the serifs of illusion. sheep metal.

knot of intention.

1052. the difference a letter trips.

a sacred grove the wound walks. the word-bed dry. to think *philosopher* of the insensible leap.

the lower path, the upper path, the known path, the unknown path.

at the graveyard, dusting snow and leaves from the four family stones, i brush away a veil between the living and the dead. hovering together, inside and outside time.

outside the grove they are climbing walls and falling.

they were speaking of their *affairs*.

sheet meddle.

torpor. trapdoor roar.

she turned to ash and He fell and fell crumpling. to the concrete cushion. cut-brow, weal-cheek, bruise-socket. pink to red to aubergine.

beauty of the healing skin. beauty of the wound.

running up the studio walls, sheep mettle.

scars that never disappear.

1064.   702 is speaking of *The Cosmic Chef: An Evening of Concrete*.

to the Pueblo people, perhaps because of the sharp contrast of black and white, it suggested dawn. the Chinese of the Manchu favoured the magpie and cherished it as an emblem of happiness.

tear-smudge. ash-rind. pen as scalpel. plough.

cast the ear so far back. listen to the ancients.

a rat in a tube placed with the opening against the victim's skin. heat applied to the closed end of the tube leaves only one path for the rat to try to escape the heat. through the victim's skin.

1069.   where is the philosopher's grove?

because he softens and drops his arms and fingers to the keys.

rocks are dancing again.

the stigmas and part of the style are picked from the saffron flower and kiln-dried between layers of paper and under the pressure of a thick board. the result is a dried *cake*.

where is *inside time?*

1074.   the automobile is a weapon of mass destruction.

one crop acre yields twenty-four pounds of the cake. four thousand three hundred and twenty flowers are required to yield one ounce of saffron. think of this the next time you eat fideua.

poet as magpie.

the chair no longer bears a body in its folds. a ghost hovers there in the shape it moulded through fifty years. all the currents of the once-living particles flow about it and settle as glimmering fading dust into its bereft brown weave.

feather nestles in a hollow among the flaxen husks.

fluttertongue 4: adagio for the pressured surround

NOTES & REFERENCES

First Epigraph:
Cixous, Hélène. *Three Steps on the Ladder of Writing* (tr. Cornell/Sellers). Columbia University Press, New York, 1993. p. 6.

Second Epigraph:
Browne, Colin. *Ground Water*. Talonbooks, Vancouver, 2002. p.176.

9.   veered. the always almost. the perilous dark.

17.   inscription in this author's copy of *A*, by Louis Zukofsky (University of California Press, Berkeley, 1978), a gift from the inscriber, bpNichol, in 1987.

33.   as a young teen he suffered from chronic mastoiditis — chronic infection of the middle ear and mastoid (a bone near the middle ear). At age 15 (1935) at Toronto Sick Children's Hospital, he had surgery which apparently removed some part of the hearing mechanism in his left ear. the result was a deaf ear.

42.   Husqvarna. just guessing. how tell one whine from another.

63.   at Bellhouse Park.

74.   September 21, 1995.

81.   Mount Galiano and Mount Sutil.

97.   to name just a few.

109.   See 97.

125.   the risk of innocence.

144.   luvox, paxil, zoloft, effexor, etc. — choice mood-lifting medications for citizens
       of the global information age in the *developed* world.

161.   see 144, 656.

165.   at the entrance, the unknown truth of encounters. a whistle may sound. a voice
       may cry out. eyes lift toward the heights.

170.   Active Pass.

174.   Gertrude.

196.   broom. a plant imported from Scotland, introduced by settlers of the Pacific
       Coast of North America. Scotch broom (cytisus scoparius) is a member of the
       Leguminosae (pulse) family now a scourge to natural plant species, though
       a relatively benign result of *developing* the globe. eradicate by digging and
       burning, then more digging and burning.

201.   August 4, 2000. Evelyn Smith.

205.   from *Torture in the Eighties*. Amnesty International Report. Dodd Mead,
       London, 1984. p.50.

209.   Eshleman, Clayton, on the writings of César Vallejo, as found in *Poems for
       the Millennium, Volume 1*. Rothenberg, J., & Joris, P. (eds.) University of
       California Press, Berkeley. p.406.

218.   i know which rock, but have been unable to find it.

249.i.   organic, preferably. see Nichol, bp. "Talking about Strawberries All of the Time" in *Martyrology Book[s] 7&*. Coach House Press, Toronto, 1990.

249.ii.   see 659.

255.   known for their nerviness.

277.   the word *horror* is afterwards and is so safe.

298.   Wah, Fred. *Faking It: Poetics and Hybridity*. (S. Kamboureli, Ed.) NeWest Press, Edmonton, 2000.

305.   Clarence Alfred Smith.

307.   just south of the Carmel Hills at el Ranchita.

313.   Wah, Fred. Various writings featuring his father, including: *Diamond Grill*, NeWest Press, Edmonton, 1996/2006 and *Waiting for Saskatchewan*, Turnstone Press, Winnipeg, 1985.

330.   Blaga, Lucian (tr. Codrescu, Andrei), from "Psalm," as appearing in *Poems for the Millennium*, Volume 1. Rothenberg, J., & Joris, P. (eds.) University of California Press, Berkeley. p.436.

332.   unattributed, as reported in *The Globe and Mail* — "Photos alleged to show torture of Iraqi POWs." May 31, 2003.

348.   Yorkville Avenue, Toronto. then a hippie and youth hangout, already going trendy. Tim Hardin, 1941-1980, died too young.

364.   Beckett, Samuel. as stated in *Dublin Magazine*, 1934 — whole phrase: *"All poetry, as distinguished from the various paradigms of prosody, is prayer."*

370.   Celan, Paul.

384.   *obbligato.* (adj.) accompanying a solo, but having a distinct character and independent importance. (n.) an obbligato part or accompaniment. Literally — obliged.

389.   for those whose words are severed.

392.   Marinetti, F.T., as found in "Manifesto of Futurism," in *Poems for the Millennium, Volume 1.* p. 198.

416.   Kroetsch, Robert. *The Hornbooks of Rita K.* University of Alberta Press, Edmonton, 2001. p. 62, 65.

428.   the wound seeks, unceasingly, its strand in the filigree of existence. then, *The Toronto Star*; now *The Globe and Mail.*

439.   police officer in Miami Dade County, speaking of "activist punks" [439.ii] at the FTAA (Free Trade Area of the Americas) Congress in Florida, November 2003, as reported in *The Globe and Mail*, November 25, 2003, in "Unlabelled" by Naomi Klein.

439.ii   police name for peaceful protesters.

457.   or look ahead to 741.

483.   *One More Chance.* hit song of the Jackson 5, on the LP *ABC.* Released May 8, 1970 (USA).

492.   Robertson, Lisa. *The Weather*. New Star Books, Vancouver, 2001. p. 29.

496.   imagine the burning flesh. too personal for further comment.

509.   named after the prison physician who invented it at Tucker State Prison Farm
        in the USA. used for several decades until the 1960s.

524.   St. Lucile Day. December 13. honours Lucy (Lucia) of Syracuse, b.283. known
        as a patron of those with haemorrhagic maladies. tortured and stabbed to death
        in 304. venerated by Catholic and Orthodox Christians. celebration also known
        as the feast of St. Lucia. as part of the feast, young Swedish girls, dressed in
        white gowns and crowned with wreaths of greenery and candles, serve coffee,
        ginger cookies (pepparkakor) and saffron bread (or buns) called lussekatter.
        for more see <www.encyclopedia4u.com/l/lucy-of-syracuse.html>, or *Flavours*
        magazine, v.2, iss.1, holiday issue, (Winnipeg) December 2004, p. 87.

542.   Robertson, Lisa. *The Weather*. New Star Books, Vancouver, 2001. p. 57.

549.   a term derived from Clarice Lispector (*O Lustro*) by Hélène Cixous. See
        Cixous' *Three Steps on the Ladder of Writing*. Columbia University Press, NY,
        1993. p.63 & elsewhere.

553.   near Highway 427 and Rathburn Road in Etobicoke, a suburb of Toronto.
        displacement.

555.   Lispector/Cixous again.

579.   dogwood, ardent in springtime. see Smith, Steven Ross. *fluttertongue 3:
        disarray,* "#21," Turnstone Press, 2005, p.12.

590.   at Earl's Restaurant, Saskatoon. March 7, 2000 about 8:52 PM.

614.   black-capped chickadee. at Willowbend near Carseland, Alberta. March 27,
        2002.

635.   also at Willowbend, March 30, 2002.

640.   diltiazem: a calcium channel blocker. calcium is involved in blood vessel contraction and in controlling the electrical impulses within the heart. by blocking calcium it relaxes and widens blood vessels and can normalize heartbeats. used to treat chest pain (angina) or high blood pressure.

645.   the Queen Mother, deceased, March 30, 2002.

656.   the names of drugs administered to cause pain or cause the limbs to writhe as a form of torture. used by the USSR and other countries in the 1980s.

659.   Low Density Lipoprotein, AKA *bad cholesterol.*

663.   ref. Nichol, bp. his word saints: St.Orm, St.Ein, St.Alwart, in a number of his books, especially *The Martyrology Books 1-9.* Coach House Press, Toronto, 1972-1993.

677.   flowers from late June to August in Saskatchewan.

678.   found in Saskatchewan in the Cypress Hills and in the foothills region

of Alberta.

695.   Oliveros, Pauline, from her theories on *Deep Listening,* stated in a variety of ways. see www.deeplistening.org/pauline.

698.   Klein, Naomi, in "Unlabelled." in *The Globe and Mail,* November 25, 2003.

702.   The gift was a boxed publication. see 1064.

703. apparently uttered simultaneously by Fred Wah at Deansheaven, Kootenay Lake, British Columbia, and Paula Jane Remlinger at St. Michael's Retreat, Lumsden, Saskatchewan, on August 2, 2003.

709. Cage, John. stated in various phrasings and in a number of places, including his Lecture on *Nothing in Silence*, Wesleyan University Press, Middleton, 1961 and various later editions, and in interview with Daniel Charles in 1968.

733. in the Strait of Georgia.

755. Sanskrit name for *bridge pose*, a yoga position that calms the brain and rejuvenates tired legs. it is a preparation for *salamba sarvagasana*, supported shoulder stand.

757. Smith, Steven Ross. "VESSEL" in *fluttertongue Book 1, the book of games*. Thistledown Press, Saskatoon, 1998. p.66.

764. Blaser, Robin. "Atlantis," in *The Holy Forest*. Coach House Press, Toronto, 1993. p. 50.

771. Schechner, Richard. *Performing Arts / 15 Journal*. Performing Arts Journal Publications, New York, 1981. p. 16.

774. Conroy, John. *Unspeakable Acts, Ordinary People*. University of California Press, Berkeley & Los Angeles, 2000. p. 11-16, 48-59, 139-157, 215-219.

806. McKinnon, Barry. *The the*. Coach House Press, Toronto, 1980.

807. Celan, Paul. *Todesfugue*. variously published and recorded. e.g. *Selected Poems and Prose of Paul Celan*, (tr. J. Felstiner), W.W. Norton, New York, London. 2001. p.30-33. the pronghorns — seen east of Medicine Hat, Alberta, on the south side of Highway 1.

809, 812. ibid, p. 67.

818.   Cixous, Hélène. *Stigmata: Escaping Texts*. Routledge, London, 1998. p.105.

820.   Appleby, Timothy. "A tyrant, yes, but he's ours." in *The Globe and Mail,* Toronto, November 16, 2002.

822.   arterial interior. as watched on the television monitor by the patient during angioplasty.

837.   (more) echoes of bpNichol.

849, 850, 851.
        Freuh, Joanna. from her performance *The Aesthetics of Orgasm*. Banff Centre for the Arts. November 21, 2002.

858.   Oliveros, Pauline. *Prayers for a Thousand Years*. Harper, San Francisco, 1999.

866.   *graupel*: granular snow pellets, soft hail.

        isocheim: an imaginary line connecting places having the same mean winter temperature.

874.   Banff, Alberta. November 2002.

897.   Lawrence, D.H. "Bavarian Gentians." From *Last Poems*, Martin Secker, London, 1933. (Bavarian gentians have blue tubular flowers)

899.   see the book of the same name: Lore, Janice *Ipsissima Verba*, Leaf Press, Lantzville, British Columbia, 2003.

907.   Smith, Steven Ross. "SNAPPY RETURN," in *Fluttertongue Book 1*. p.104. self-referentiality? self-indulgence? isn't it all? yet there is a reach, a tendency to fall.

922.   Kroetsch, Robert. "The Ledger" in *Completed Field Notes*. University of Alberta Press, Edmonton, 2000. p. 21.

940.   Emmett H Robinson Smith.

957.   (on reading and trying to comprehend) Levinas, Emmanuel, *entre nous: Thinking-of-the-Other*. Columbia University Press, New York, 1998.

962.   Gunnars, Kristjana. *The Silence of the Country*. Coteau Books, Regina, 2002. p. 10.

964.   Filson tin packer hat.

971.   Cage, John 1968. *Reunion*.
        this piece was performed in 1968 at Ryerson Polytechnical Institute (alma mater of S.R. Smith, gr. 1968) in Toronto. Lowell Cross constructed a chess board equipped with photoreceptors that served as a gating mechanism to transmit or cut off sound produced by other musicians and to control lights. John Cage and Marcel Duchamp played a game of chess. other participants included Teeny Duchamp, David Tudor, Gordon Mumma, and David Behrman. the book *Marcel Duchamp and John Cage* by Shigeko Kubota (1970) contains photographs and a recording of this performance. (this description found at John Greschak's website: *Connections between Music and Chess* at www.greschak.com/muschess.htm)

975.   ref. computer art projects of British artist Jane Prophet; see *Decoy* and other works at http://www.janeprophet.co.uk.

977.   *paude arara* tr. *parrot's perch*. (Chile, prior to 1982). the victim, usually naked, is trussed into a crouching position with the arms hugging the legs. a pole is passed through the narrow gap between the bent knees and elbows, the ends of the pole resting on two trestles or desks, with the victim hanging head down. electric current is then administered to the various parts of the body, and water squirted at high pressure into the mouth and nose until the victim is on the verge of suffocation. see *Torture in the Eighties*, p. 151.

981.   some materials throughout are recycled. others are recyclable.

987.   Zukofsky, Louis. *A. 8*. University of California Press, Berkeley, 1978. p.56.

996.   Spring Valley Ranch near the Saskatchewan Cypress Hills, April 2002.

1003.   not yet.

1010.   Deleuze, G., Parnet, C., *Dialogues*. (tr. Tomlinson, H. & Habberjam, B.)
        Columbia University Press, New York. p.65.

1012.   words/wounds/wonders/wails may be closer than they seem.

1013.   Shikatani, Gerry. Poet and gourmand. see *A Passion for Food*. The Mercury
        Press, Toronto, 2000; *Aqueduct*, Mercury/Underwhich/Wolsak and Wyun,
        Toronto, 1996; *Lake and other Stories*, The Mercury Press, Toronto, 1996, and
        other books. four diners were served at a comfortable and well-appointed table.

1019.   Sallot, Jeff. *At home, Arar still haunted by anger and fear.* in *The Globe and
        Mail*, Toronto, November 6, 2003.

1025.   of the saffron plant.

1032.   on a trail near Banff, at a dry branch of the Bow River, November 2002.

1049.   Hejinian, L. *The Composition of the Cell* in *The Cold of Poetry*. Sun & Moon
        Press, Los Angeles, 1994. p. 113.

1050.   Szeto, Rebecca, San Francisco visual artist. visit http://www.rebeccaszeto.com,
        and see *Herd Mentality* in her portfolio. These images were first encountered
        by the author in Szeto's studio exhibition called *Counting Sheep* at the Banff
        Centre for the Arts in 2002.

1052.   see 1050, 1058.

1064.   nichol, bp. *The Concrete Chef: An Evening of Concrete*. Oberon Press, Ottawa,
        1970.

1069.   wherever you wish, not far from the dancing rocks.

1074.   one million people die in automobile accidents per year worldwide. three
         million die from the effects of air pollution.

The Bindery
Shane Rhodes

This much-anticipated third collection from acclaimed poet Shane

Rhodes is full of poems to be felt, to be underlined, to be whispered, to be dog-eared and talked about. Tracing themes of travel, love, personal and collective history, *The Bindery* combines lyrical poetry with experimental verve. The title poem of the book, a remarkable long poem, is a rich collage of lyrical and prose poems with haiku, philosophical meditations, aphorisms, and photographs. These poems were composed from hurried scribbles in Mexican bus stations, meditations on street corners in Buenos Aires, letters from friends in the Himalaya, and odes from the Canadian hinterland, and emphasize how "to be stained by what we see."

ISBN 10: 1-897126-14-X • ISBN 13: 978-1-897126-14-1

$16.95 CDN • $12.95 US

Available through your favourite bookseller

Vancouver Walking
Meredith Quartermain

Journey along Vancouver's colourful city streets, past its landmarks,

through the sounds and smells of Chinatown. Ramble along the seawall on English Bay, ride the curving streets to Kitsilano on a winter afternoon, and experience the vibrant sights and sounds of the city's history as it jostles for a place in the present. *Vancouver Walking* is a collection of descriptive poetry that evokes visions of Vancouver and the history that haunts it. Meredith Quartermain paints sharp, simple, and often ironic impressions of the city, completing her collection with a train journey down the west coast and inland over the Sierra Nevada to Utah and Colorado.

ISBN 10: 1-896300-81-2 • ISBN 13: 978-1-896300-81-8

$14.95 CDN • $9.95 US

Winner of the 2006 Dorothy Livesay Poetry Award

ACKNOWLEDGEMENTS

The author wishes to acknowledge opportunities that enabled the development and refinement of this manuscript: The Saskatchewan Arts Board, Individual Assistance Grant, 2002, 2004; Willowbend, near Carseland, Alberta, spring 2002 and winter 2007; The Writers' and Artists' Colony at Christopher Lake (program of the Saskatchewan Writers Guild), September 2002; The Leighton Studio, Banff Centre for the Arts, November, 2002; El Ranchita, near Humboldt, Saskatchewan, spring 2003; the Sage Hill Writing Experience Fall Poetry Colloquium, Lumsden, Saskatchewan, 2003; and various sojourns on Galiano Island, British Columbia, between 2000 and 2002 (location of the philosopher's grove and the forking cedar). A grateful nod to Katherine Melnyk and Alice Moulding at NeWest Press, and to J. Jill Robinson for their work in the final stages. Special thanks to Fred Wah and Douglas Barbour for their editorial dedication.

STEVEN ROSS SMITH was born in Toronto and raised in the Parkdale neighbourhood of Toronto. In 1986 Smith discovered Saskatchewan at a writing retreat at St. Peter's Abbey in Muenster. Shortly afterwards he moved from Toronto to Saskatoon to devote more time to writing. Smith has written eleven books, and contributed to many periodicals and anthologies. He has also contributed to the literary community by working as a Program Manager for the Saskatchewan Writers Guild and as the Business Manager of *Grain Magazine*, as well as the Executive Director of the Sage Hill Writing Experience. Smith creates, records, and performs sound poetry. Previous works include *Pliny's Knickers* (with Hilary Clark and Betsy Rosenwald), which won the bpNichol Chapbook Award 2005, and *Fluttertongue 3: disarray*, which won the Book of the Year Prize in the Saskatchewan Book Awards 2005. *adagio for the pressured surround* is the fourth book in Smith's *Fluttertongue* series. He currently lives in Saskatoon, Saskatchewan, with his wife Jill and son Emmett.